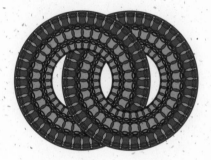

AN APRON FULL OF
Beans
NEW AND SELECTED POEMS

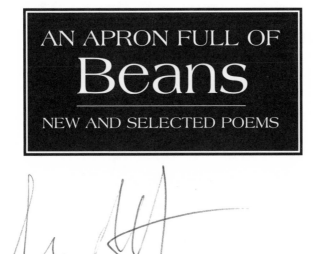

AN APRON FULL OF
Beans

NEW AND SELECTED POEMS

Sam Cornish

CavanKerry ⬧ Press LTD.

Library of Congress Cataloging-in-Publication Data

Cornish, Sam.
An apron full of beans: new and selected poems / Sam Cornish.—1st ed.
p. cm.
ISBN-13: 978-1-933880-09-9
ISBN-10: 1-933880-09-0
1. African Americans—Poetry. I. Title.

PS3553.O68A82 2008
811'.54—c22

2008020545

Cover art, Oscar Astromujoff © 2008
Author photograph by Jon Strymish
Cover and book design by Peter Cusack

First Edition 2008
Printed in the United States of America

CavanKerry Press Ltd.
Fort Lee, New Jersey
www.cavankerrypress.org

NOTABLE ◈ VOICES

CavanKerry Press is proud to publish the works
of established poets of merit and distinction.

CavanKerry Press is grateful for the
support it receives from the
New Jersey State Council on the Arts.

Acknowledgments

Some of these poems were previously published in *Folks Like Me, To Cross a Parted Sea, 1935, Generations, Sam's World, Songs of Jubilee*, and *Sometimes*.

I wish to acknowledge the assistance and editorial support of Florella Orowan.

Thanks to Baron Wormser for sound criticism and advice.

OTHER BOOKS

by

SAM CORNISH

To Cross a Parted Sea
Folks Like Me
1935: A Prose Memoir
Songs of Jubilee: New & Selected Poems
Sam's World—Poems
Generations—Poems
Grandmother's Pictures—Children's Book
Your Hand in Mine—Children's Book
Chicory—Anthology, co-edited with Lucien Dixon

PAMPHLETS

Sometimes
Winters
In This Corner
People Beneath the Window

For our Mothers & Friends:

Harriet Cook
Cora Cook
Phillis Wheatley
Wilma Stang
Evelyn Levy
Ernestine Rouse
Marie Tervalon
Mary Edsall
Lillian Barbour
Louise Bowman

CONTENTS

THE WORLD OF (SOME OF) OUR FATHERS

HOGMEAT

FRANKIE HAS A SONG FOR YOU

INTRODUCTION

In *An Apron Full of Beans* one sees all the facets of Sam Cornish's mature work. In many poems the reader encounters a profound engagement with history that is almost Brechtian in that not only does Cornish take up iconic figures, such as Paul Robeson, Harriet Tubman, and Frederick Douglass, but also he uses unnamed historic actors as the motors of events that the iconic figures come to embody. He also frequently displays a sometimes touching, sometimes hilarious feeling for popular culture, especially music, sports, the movies, and literature so that the historical figures mix with filmic characters played by Jim Brown, Louise Beavers, Dorothy Dandridge, and Robert De Niro as well as fictional figures, such as Richard Wright's Bigger Thomas and Chester Himes's Coffin Ed Johnson and Gravedigger Jones.

Cornish has described his artistic journey as being "from Beat to African American." This description is apt. If we take "Beat" to mean the literary counterculture of the 1950s and 1960s, or what was sometimes called the New American Poetry, and not simply the circle of artists around Allen Ginsburg and Jack Kerouac, then it is true that Cornish, like many black writers of his generation, served a literary apprenticeship in that counterculture. However, if I were going to connect Cornish's work displayed in *An Apron Full of Beans* to any particular school of the literary counterculture of the 1950s and 1960s, I would say that it is closer in spirit to the poets of the Black Mountain School, with their concern with history (especially local history) and voice or to those of the New York School with their interest in popular culture than it is to the work of the Beats. Still, to connect Cornish's work to the Beats in the broad sense of the literary counterculture of his youth does help one understand the origins of his poetry in some important ways. And if we take "African American" or "Black" to be a sort of shorthand for the explosion of socially engaged African-American art that was so closely tied to the Black Power movement of the 1960s and 1970s as to be inseparable from it, it is also true that Cornish's arrival as a mature artist occurred during this period and his work engaged both the aesthetics and the institutions of the Black Arts Movement.

Being "Beat," again in the larger sense, in Cornish's hometown of Baltimore was not precisely the same as being "Beat" in New York City, Los Angeles, or San Francisco. The literary counterculture in Baltimore was obviously a smaller community, removed from the prominent institutions of the movement, such as City Lights Books, Totem-Corinth Books, *Yugen* magazine, *Origins* magazine, and so on. This had its good and bad aspects for a developing poet, I suspect. I am sure that it was not possible to forget about being black anywhere in the United States for any length of time. However, the palpable history of slavery in Baltimore, where Frederick Douglass had labored as a slave, and the living presence of Jim Crow in Maryland, a state in which African diplomats were still regularly denied service as they drove between New York and Washington during the early 1960s, were not quite the same as in New York or Boston, where the history of slavery is often literally buried (as in the slave cemeteries that have been recently unearthed in New York) and the rules of segregation were somewhat different, if famously intense, particularly at the time Cornish moved to Boston in the 1970s. Thanks to Douglass, the Eastern Shore of Maryland and Baltimore were early memorialized as literary epicenters of slavery—something of which Cornish is acutely aware:

frederick douglass did you see your mother
did you know the woman in the dark
who said she was your mother
who said she was your mother
is this the woman you remember
the woman you saw only twice

Baltimore was also a complex city in Cornish's youth because it combined something of the character of an old southern urban center, like Charleston or Savannah, and that of a moderm industrial city, like Pittsburgh or Detroit, ranging from the Peabody Institute in Mount Vernon to the Bethlehem Steel plant at Sparrow's Point. That is to say that one might trace practically the entire history of African Americans in the United States, and their resistance to oppression, from the slave era through Reconstruction, the onset of Jim Crow, the Garvey movement, the New

Negro Renaissance, the radical political and cultural movements of the 1930s and 1940s, the civil rights movement, Black Arts, and Black Power, to the largely dismal postindustrial urban present ("I came to the Communist Party, with Bessie Smith, Karl Marx, and Marcus Garvey on my mind"). Again, Cornish's artistic apprenticeship took place in a counterculture in Baltimore when bohemians interacted with Communists, where the mimeographed chapbooks and magazines of bohemia intersected with the new journals, books, and broadsides of Black Arts.

I mention these things because I think they help frame our understanding of both the typicality and the distinctiveness of Cornish's work in *An Apron Full of Beans*. Again, whether one is talking about Amiri Baraka, Larry Neal, Sonia Sanchez, Ishmael Reed, David Henderson, Calvin Hernton, Ed Bullins, and so on, an apprenticeship in an artistic counterculture where bohemian artists, the Old Left, the New Left, and black nationalists intermingled was a very common story for writers more or less of Cornish's generation. Cornish's move from the interiority and the self-referential, almost private diction of his earliest published poems in the 1960s to the far more direct style that has continued to characterize his mature work, too, is something that one might detect in different ways among many writers of the Black Arts era.

Yet surprisingly, given the emphasis of Malcolm X and other avatars of Black Arts and Black Power on knowing and understanding history, Cornish is virtually unique among Black Arts era poets, other than the elder poetic statesman Robert Hayden, in the way he draws directly from African American, history from slavery through civil rights, Black Power, and beyond, often in lyric cycles. Sometimes these poems or series of poems take up well-known figures, as in the Nat Turner poems in this volume. Sometimes Cornish's poems center on family members or unnamed black everypeople drawn with sharp historical specificity despite their typicality— as seen in the black Communists that are the speakers in "Ebony" and "Annals of the Poor." For the most part, he avoids the sort of mythic or ritual history that marked much Black Arts poetry and drama, although his work was a forerunner of later verse by black authors that deeply engages history, if in different ways, say Rita Dove's *Thomas and Beulah* or Kevin Young's *To Repel Ghosts*. Or if he presents a certain mythic pattern, he suggests that it resides in everyday life, and the history of everyday people, so to speak, as well as that of better-known figures. And, while I hesitate to comment too definitively about the source of Cornish's poetry and poetics, I would tentatively suggest that perhaps it is the result of being Beat and black in Baltimore, with its particular history and character, that have helped produce the distinctiveness and distinction of Cornish's poetry. One of the wonderful things about Cornish's poetry is the way it balances this history with a sort of spare, but distinctive voice. I mentioned the Black Mountain School earlier, but unlike, say much of the work of Robert Creeley or Denise Levertov (if you want to connect her to Black Mountain), where the focus on the paring down of language threatens to overwhelm the subject, or the work of Ed Dorn and Charles Olson, where a certain recondite style sometimes obscures history, Cornish manages to beautifully harmonize between voice and history. And like poets of the New York School, particularly Frank O'Hara, Cornish creates poetic landscapes that draw deeply on popular culture, especially film. Although like O'Hara's, these popular culture landscapes are often intensely personal, they also look outward, now perhaps resembling Amiri Baraka in poems like "Masked Angel Costume: The Sayings of Mantan Moreland," and deeply engage history. Such poems as "Carmen Jones" and the goofily wonderful "Mars Attacks" remind us that films, recorded music, and literary works like Richard Wright's *Native Son* and the essays of James Baldwin are historical events, too:

Carmen's mouth is painted

red
but sun and God

have made her
brown

not afraid of sin
or the South

fuck Mississippi

and the Klan

life is short
and morning

(in a colored town)
comes too soon

James E. Smethurst, PhD
University of Massachusetts, Amherst

AN APRON FULL OF BEANS

PICTURES OF MY MOTHER

The pictures of my mother
Never look like me

They are my ancestors
With an apron

Full of beans a mouth
Ready to speak

I am still waiting
To hear their voices

SAM CORNISH

IN MR. SANDERS' BARBERSHOP

For my mother, who got my first haircut at Mr. Sanders'

sit down   tell us a story   this Saturday morning
now the week's almost done   chew some
tobacco   light a Camel take a deep smoke
in Mr. Sanders' barber chair
(you almost own it payin' and tippin')
gettin' that hair cut tha's right   put your behind
here in Mr. Sanders' chair him with the gentle touch
(ask the women)   he makes your nappy
hair lay down straight   go through the comb
drift to the floor   Mr. Sanders tell stories
of hard work   this week done you out
those hands are rock hard   grippin' that broom
you with the red cap on   so tired of standin'
at the train liftin' bags or fine clothing
young man says Mr. Sanders "I know
your mamma and you workin' so hard
sit down tell me your story"

BEING IN A BOX IS BETTER THAN

DYING LIKE JESUS

THE RIVER JUST KEEPS ON GOING

Huck Finn redhead Huck Finn
with the devil in him
white boy with a fishin' pole
and a Nigger friend named Jim
good friend although a Nigger
thinks Huck but Huck's a boy
Jim's a man
Huck smokes a pipe
skips school and loves the drifting river
going places other towns
the Mississippi is the river
of Huck and Jim friends on the water
Huck is Mr. and Jim is Nigger
looking for the North
it is the end of the river
says Huck but Jim knows the river
just keeps on going

FANNY KEMBLE

up and down
the river
listening to

the banjo
black
men singing
rowing

up and down
the river

Fanny Kemble
heard the blues

HUNGRY

Nat Turner his blood is on the corn
His number on the leaves
Nat Turner
Slave
Composer
Man
Death
And darkness

IN MR. TURNER'S FIELDS

Property of Massa Benjamin
I still learned to read

Beside my plough
I prayed and waited

Blacks have always trusted
Me for I have always waited

For a sign
I heard a loud move

In the heavens
The serpent

Was loose
Christ has laid down the yoke

THE TIME IS DRAWING NEAR

Farmers and slaves saw
Nat dead overseers wished
He had fled to Ohio
Hymnbook in his hand
White women dreamed
Of him with sword and Bible
Running
Through the South
Chanting death chanting
Neither men nor women shall be spared

PREACHER NAT

Preacher Nat came with a sword, a book and the Word; the Word was the sword.

If I had my way,
If I had my way,
If I had my way
I'd tear this building down.

Nat had his way. When dead, he was a ghost when the moon was rising. He was a meeting when a white man was not present. He was the water that made them free. Nat was books, and Bibles burned. Any man or woman teaching a slave to read was following Nat's sword.

Some people went back to Jesus, to Nat and Jesus, but Jesus brought the body out of itself through suffering.

Sometimes, voices came from Jesus and Nat:

"Go back," said Jesus
"Steal away," said Nat

There were places deep and dark, that Jesus could not reach. There were men like Frederick Douglass, who did not believe that death was freedom, or that Jesus could talk about property. There were women who ran away and came back. Women who were like Harriet Tubman, so that God could use them.

HARRIET TUBMAN

Lord
While I sow earth

Or song
The sun goes

Down   my only
Mother

On a dirt floor
Is dying

Hair falling
From her head

Mouth open
On straw and dirt

Mother's only memories
The smell of stew

And chicken
Boiling in a pot

The children
Made in her

And sold
She moves only

When I come in
From the fields

She knows
I live her life
Jesus you hid

Behind the good
Book

And its words
I sing

And dance to conceal
The pistol

Under my apron

HARRIET TUBMAN IS MOSES

Harriet Tubman is General Moses
Moses is coming
Let the moon rise
For the Lord
Moses is coming   and I
Have been waiting
Moses is coming
Heard stomping the darkness
Coming to set her children free

FINDING THE RAILROAD
WITH MY FEET

My master
When drunk would beat
Whip
This passenger Philip Hart
I took this train
My master wrote
Runaway large scar
On his forehead Philip Hart
Part of his toe
Cut off
I met another Negro
Man named Joe
Scar on his toe
Took the train
The long black train
Heading north
Our feet the railroad

MY FATHER STOLE AWAY

My father brings me
Gifts
Of melon
Parched
Corn
My father stole away
Stole
Away north
My grandfather
Gave
His son
A handful
Of
Parched
Corn
Told
Him
To steal
Away
He ain't
Got long
To stay
Here

My grandfather
Prayed
To gods
Living
In Africa
To God
And
His son

To let my father
Steal
Away

My father
Sang
The songs
Of slaves
Of friends
And families
My father
Sings
No more
My father
Stole away

JOHN BROWN

John Brown
met black
men all his life
his eyes
blue grey
hair growing
low on his forehead
spent his day
behind plough
and Bible
walked twelve
miles on
meals of potatoes
and cabbage soup

THE OVERLAND MAIL

being in a box is better
than dying
like Jesus
being
in a box two feet eight
inches deep
leaving Richmond
without worrying
going
through the woods looking
for a light and waiting
or

hiding in a
cellar
so
I just stepped
inside a box
mailed it to a Friend*
and left going
Overland Mail to Philadelphia

* Quaker

WOMAN IN A RED DRESS

In a red dress a woman

On her knees washes
A floor one hundred years ago

She is shaping the life
Of her children   she thinks

As a woman   of freedom
A dark place in the woods

Where the North enters the trees
She wonders if her life is history

A woman losing her children
If reading is a crime

She does not ask for pity
There is a damp rag on the floor

In the dress she slept
In   the dress

She had her children in
She scrubs the floor

Does not brush her teeth
She picks them with straw or sticks

She moves on her knees
Watch the ceiling in the water

Reflected in the water
Everything in her life

Is hard like the floor
She washes

The water is in her hands
The water is between her legs

Her body is like a sack of muscle
Her hands are dark with water

She wonders about her children
How many children

If she could count past her fingers
About her body

The words she would find
If she could read

She gathers water
Like sounds in her head

She kneels
Like a slave

In church
Like a slave preparing

To dance
In front of the big house

She pretends to be quiet
She is grinding glass

Pissing
In the evening

Meal

HARRIET BRINGS RUNAWAYS NORTH

Harriet Tubman trampin' out
of the wilderness
Leaning on the Lord
Get ready for Harriet she
Comes in the night

Harriet sings only twice

Harriet takes you
Where the rain can't wet you
No sun to burn you
When Harriet sings
Runaway it's safe
Harriet
We will follow you
To the grave
Harriet
Journeying North
Walk them easy
Don't leave them
Behind

FREDERICK DOUGLASS

frederick douglass did you see your mother
did you know the woman in the dark
who said she was your mother
who said she was your mother
is this the woman you remember
the woman you saw only twice
the woman who walked all night

                         who walked all night
to see her son   the mother
                      walked all night
frederick douglass did you see your mother
did you know the woman
who said she was your mother

how did she know you
how did she know you
did she know you in the dark
did she know the touch of your face
did she know the dark of your face
did she say to herself
this is my son
this is my son

                  frederick
                  frederick douglass did you see
your mother

would you know your mother
would you know your mother
now that you are old
now that you are old
would you know the woman who said

i am your mother
the woman who walked all night
who walked all night
frederick douglass did you see your mother
did you know the woman in the dark

WHILE LINCOLN IS STILL THINKING

They baked the bread
bless their souls
raised children
broke the ground
like a plough
were the people
(no melting pot
farthest down)
they built the houses
shod the horses
they were the people
thousands gone
they sang
oh give Jesus
in that morning
when the lamp
burns low
run nigger run
when the lamp
is burned
down low   you baked
as you worked
broke (a dime
never stayed
in your pockets)
raised their children
loved sometimes
your own
(old lonesome road)
while Lincoln (bless
his ol'
soul)   is still thinking
run nigger run

RUNAWAY SONG

bird in the air
eyes above the trees
Negro goes north

AGE

age
is for those
with fathers

my mother
lived twelve
miles
distant
she was
my last
place

ALMOST GONE

I think
Of the folks
And home
And lift my tired and broken
Feet
With a song
From a weary throat
That blesses the sun
Creates
The thirst
And fire
I sit down
A spell
Then rest
And feed
For another
Day is getting
Ready to come

RIVERS TO CROSS

MAN WITH THE DEVIL ON HIS TAIL

For Robert Johnson and David Smith

Red Bone's in town
tall lanky Red Bone

guitar and blues
man devil's not

far behind when
Red Bone hits town

five string guitar
fingers lickin' up

some blues he is
a man gone wrong

Red Bone brings
on Saturday night

throw some coins
in his hat he'll

give a tune do it
now not much

time for Red Bone
devil's not far

behind never look
back unless you

want to see the fire
on your tail says

Red Bone guitar
man long man

blues man apricot
or paper bag brown

that my man Mr.
Bones giving us a

tune for a nickel
a dime a glass

of lemonade for
a man with the devil

on his tail

BIG BOY* LEAVES HOME

the good people the honest men and women
the fathers brought their sons   women spread

picnic blankets   the men gathered twigs for small
fires of Mississippi sang "Gather at the river

the beautiful beautiful river" the thin mean people
hard times living in their white faces

hung Big Boy let him twist and sway
with the rope they educated the people of Nigger Town

after they the church going white
people who read and memorized the Testament

kept the Sabbath picked apples
for the children

(this was an outing on a farm)
for the friends that were not there

they took screwdrivers and bore ribbons
of flesh with dull kitchen knives   tried to cut

fingers from Big Boy's (tough and nasty
nigger still living) hand and someone

at last   cut off a finger (let him hang)
angry when Big Boy

* Character and voices are based on a Richard Wright short story "Big Boy Leaves Home" and other documents.

35

would not be   still
(don't swear in front of the children)

they started a little fire
(niggers make me hungry)

under him
smoking Big Boy smelled

like a church picnic
yams fresh slaughtered pig   pork

as the meat is turned
over

again and a little sauce is added
and turned

again till both sides an even brown
after Big Boy was dark and crisp

and the shoes
and fingernails

the ribbons
of flesh were collected in

purses pockets
little sacks with apples

and left over
chicken and bowls of potato salad

someone noticed
it had begun to rain

sheltered the women
with coats and blankets

lifted arms against
the sudden gust of wind

and cold rain

A PHOTOGRAPH OR TWO

*Based on photos from "Wisconsin Death Trip" **

these are the family histories in the box camera
the false fronts of main street

the common death of the everyday towns
a "Negro" cutting hair in his barbershop

kiss the flag   nigger
so mysterious now

this simple America nobody remembers
but tramps living the hard times in freight cars

colored ladies eating oysters sitting on chairs in front
of their cabins and shacks

talking about a "Negro" farmer beaten
by the neighborhood Christians with a poker

* A book of photographs by Michael Lesy published in 1973 depicting the
inhabitants of Black River Falls, Wisconsin, during the Great Depression of the 1890s.

APRICOT BRIGHT AND TAN

The sleeping car porters
Negro
men on the railroad
some were doctors
lawyers
shining
black
their faces miles of white
teeth so beautiful brown and black
tan and apricot bright like bananas
skin like baked potato smiling years of serving
from Alabama to Baltimore
believed in the church of Jesus
white Baptists and
black

EBONY

My father labored
in the mine his
hands blacker than
his face
face as black
as
coal   his hands
darkest
coal dust
my mother
a fair skinned
woman   former
schoolteacher
worked at home
read the Bible
and prayed &
I became
a Communist

MY OLD GAL MY HONEY

some us are old like that woman
chewin' tobacco the porch creakin'

under her rocking chair
but that honeybee goes the song

don't sting nobody but me

LIVER LIPS

When I say I am a jazz man, the question is always asked if I made
records, or did you play with so-and-so? Well, I done had my share
of bad gin, been married, had hard luck though she more than me,
worked as a porter and played my cornet in speakeasies, roadhouses.
Others say I am a jazz singer, a dark-complexioned man with a
harsh voice, sound down-home to some, bad to others when I sing
"The Sun Is Gonna Shine on My Back Door Someday." It's my voice
that tells you I think better times is coming to men working in the
mine, women loving the men who work in the mine, the sharecropper with his miserable shanty that is not his home, and the land
that he works that belongs to the white man, to the strikers who
protested and marched against the nightstick. The sun is going to
shine on men in the soup lines and the cook that stirs the soup and
makes it thin to serve more and more and even more in the kitchen,
to feed the hungry. When you listen to a record over and over
again, the sun gonna shine in my back door someday.

WORKERS OF THE SOIL

In memory of Robert W. Lee of the New Era
Bookstore, Baltimore

I am a Negro worker   these
Are my hands (like marching feet)
The hands of a working Negro
I am not an educated man
But a worker of the soil   the South land
Is a hunger in my body   now thin
And early   to the streets looking
For work these are the words
Of an undetected man
A working man
A Negro man

CHOCOLATE

Color
This man
Sweet
As candy
'Cause
Solid
Black
Ain't
Worth
Shit

TOOMER'S GONE

say
good-bye

Harlem
Jean

Toomer's
fled down

town
Nigger

moon
burning

Jean
says

good-bye
Harlem

down
like

dusk
skin

so fair
Jean

is down
town

SAM CORNISH

almost
white

ol'
southern

road
sweet

as cane
Toomer's

gone now
no nickel-

and-dime
spittoons

rent parties
and dreambooks

Harlem jive
no more

no more
Marcus Garvey

go back to Africa
on the Steamship

Wheatley

Jean's going
downtown

SEWER

In Harlem
(the Negro
capital) not
a cot
in this hotel
is worth
a dime

HIS FINGERS SEEM TO SING

In the South
Where I was born   color
Bars and Jim Crow cars
Fine brown skin girls
Sang and black men danced
In their dark faces
The merry and dangerous
Whites of their eyes
I was young and made
My music beating
On hat boxes
My music was color blind
I traveled with my gin
A quart of whiskey a day
And ice
Across a country black
And white played on the streets
Where policemen walked in groups
And Fats Waller   sat
At the piano
His fingers seemed to sing
And so did Negro America
Through rural towns with moonshine
And poor whites
riots and thoughts of war
The music was swing
And radio was the voice
That brought us together
My music was color blind
For fine young men in zoot suits
And brown skinned girls

PITCHER OF LEMONADE

PITCHER OF LEMONADE

For Cora Keyes

St. Louis child black
Face shining like sunflowers

And daffodils
Laughing on the fence

White woman's child you are
A pitcher of lemonade golden child

Your eyes were blue
Still a nigger the lord will provide

Little high brown boy
Grandmother's favorite child

SAM CORNISH

UNCLES

For Herbert and Eddie

Lord take away
the weather in his bones so
all of them teeth can make a smile
he is a Baptist and can almost
break your heart
in the living room at the kitchen table
life is hard and the living
is where he finds it
uncle has a spittoon and ashtray
has arms where I can hide and smile and cry
smokes a fine big cigar   almost a father
(and to some he is) uncles brothers of mothers
and fathers and friend of mine   uncles black
and brown (some are yeller) married to sisters
men of the family strong as a big coal truck
at ballgames and barber
shops   work in factories, grocery stores and liquor
stores takes the elevator up faster
than young feet on the stair
uncle was a sharecropper   from Alabama Mississippi
Virginia Rising Sun Maryland has paychecks and
Superman comic books comes equipped
with walks (and hugs) thick porkchops from the butcher
shop and pints of Pikesville whiskey for himself
and Kosher wine sweet for Grandmother
because it's Jewish is good
dark and thick Shapiro Concord grape

Uncle carries a pistol and his friends call him Jim
say he sings like the Inkspots

with their ringed fingers and deep
Southern voices   not wanting
to set the world on fire
he just makes a woman's heart
smoke (a little) and cuss
the winter and the lonely life
my uncle with a strap put the fear
of God into my behind and nasty mouth
because I talked back to my mother
his sister his friend
he teaches first grade
in summer softball
now rides the rails serving
sandwiches and coffee
and shines shoes so black
they shine   and say sugar daddy
'cause he pays
the rent brings soul food on Sunday
and a dime for me
before dinner bowing his head to lead
the table in thanks
in Jesus' name Amen
uncles smell of smoke
and soap and work   dancing and laughing
away trouble   uncles
voices (is a drum) like hunger
laughter like lightly falling rain
thick fingers
and hands like
hunks of meat they are
family
when the father is dead
or walked away
all the men we want our fathers to be
all the men (I hope) we are

DEEP CHOCOLATE

For Donald Jerome and all the long bad boys
For the Inkspots

Colored
Boys:
Sounding
Like the
Sweetest
Chocolate
Colored
Boys
Long
Legged
Colored
Boys
Brown
Skinned
Boys
No
Good
Ever
Loving
Bowlegged
Colored
Boys
Home
Boys
Smelling
Soul
Food
Jailbirds
Mama's boys

With bad
And greasy
Mops
Swaying
To a little
Bebop
Black boys writing
Black
Southern
Black
Boy
Shining
Like
Fine
Sunday
Shoes

SAM CORNISH

HERE COMES SUNDAY MORNING

Here comes
The band marching
The neighbors friends and shopkeepers stand
Up and down the street
Look at what that drum majorette can do
John Philip Sousa is
Deep somewhere in the
Drum the marching feet—
This ain't Saturday night blues
But the Sunday morning parade
Drumbeats loud
Over the bar and dinner
Tables—the churches are emptied out
Those fine colored boys and girls
Old colored men
Pimping in white
For Sunday morning's
Coming down the street

HAVE YOU HEARD THE LITTLE PRESBYTERIAN CHILDREN SING?

Have you heard the little
Presbyterian children sing
such dignity
dressed and starched
in gowns
of black
and white
little girls wearing
gloves
little ladies
on Sundays
brats
all week   ask their teacher
and those boys fine
and dressed like little undertakers
black suits and shoes
white shirts and socks
when they stand and sing proud as the finest house
giving welcome
to Sunday morning
little brown and black boys and girls
praising the morning   listen to them sing

SAM CORNISH

SOONER OR LATER

sooner or later
somebody dies
in your family
& you got to know
what to do
or you are going
to feel bad
when the women
pull out
their handkerchiefs
& your hands
are still
in your pockets

58

WHEN MY GRANDMOTHER DIED

when
my
grandmother
died

a black
bird
was
lost
inside
the
house

BROTHERMAN

For Herman Cornish

Was never a boy
But always a son

His education
On the street

Let his dukes
Do his talking

Wore mean
Threads

Keep a steady
Eye and seek

You shall find
Said brother

Man   quick
With the dukes

King
Of the avenue

WITH A WORD ON MY LIPS, *I FIGHT*

SINCE I HAVE SEEN YOU

Something brought the men
of my generation
out of the rolling dark
southern towns
the cities   and rows
of tenement shacks where the names
of generations
of Italians   and Irish
names were written beneath
the wallpaper of the rooms
which stayed as they
moved on and
closed the cities against
us into north ends
little Italian rows
of marble steps in Polish
ghettoes in Baltimore

something from the labor
the lynchings and boss men
with their promises
and of work brought me
to Communism   white
boys talked of the people
living in boxcars with the promises
of Herbert Hoover

I knuckled around
the jails and towns
talked about my hard
times in the Baptist church
when the choir sang

help me cross the river
we ended
our song still on the other
side waiting for the
sun to shine waiting for
the word the presence

way in the middle
of the air   the promise of sorrow
songs held not the truth
of the white boys in the Communist
party   bringing me drunk
without a dime for this job
bringing my people the street
to march to strike

ANNALS OF THE POOR

I came to the Communist Party with Bessie Smith,
Karl Marx, and Marcus Garvey on my mind. I had
known the third degree, death row, the back rooms of
local police stations, shotgun in one hand, book in the
other, firm in my resolve to stand up for my people. I
joined the party in '35, year of the black storms; our
freedom like something blowing in the trees. I was
despondent as dusk, full mouth; lips like a thick slice
of folded liver, grim as the blackness which was my
father's face, as unfortunate as the children of Ham,
who laughing at their father's nakedness, became what
my father called the "cursed race." I am (I like my
father) a brute broad of mouth, sagging eyes, a back of
muscle bent through work, and terrible posture, less a
man, more a mule. A cruel man called Mississippi,
made terrible by life, named after the awful river. Life
like the angry Mississippi was the death and destruc-
tion of Negro song, in the flood uprooting houses and
trees tearing through the community the lives of its
useless people. My father was a man of harsh words and
fierce anger. In my blood the darkness, the temper of
my father flows but in my head the words the thoughts
of something gentle and unforgiving as the intellect of
my mother. I came to the party my mother's son with a
word on my I lips "I fight." Fight Nigger and fight she
did and here I come because my mother was a woman
fighting, a woman whose life was her sons and my
father. I came to the party, a fist, a mind, a man. I came
because there was nowhere else to go.

MISSISSIPPI

we moved from one
land
to another

my sister died
crossing the river

the cradle
on your mother's
back
is empty

& the water
rises

mother
why did we go on
if we were dying

    your father carried
    a fish over his back
    its tail touched the ground

    grandmother
    used to chain herself
    to the post office
    for women's rights

PICTURE OF MY GRANDFATHER

The army makes men
Of slaves my grandfather
Wore a uniform at Tuskegee
Years after the war

SAM CORNISH

WHY I DID NOT GIVE MY SEAT TO
THAT WHITE MAN IN 1932

I am a working woman
an all-
day woman
my hands are stones
that beat
these clothes to white
sweat burns
my hips
churn and thrust
my breasts
have weaned
the South
my feet kept
moving long
after sun-
rise and the moon
followed
me my old feet
my old feet
buried within my shoes
my head
is a southern tongue
my heart is the Scottsboro
boy   telling
his story
a tale longer
than the history
this woman has seen before she came home back
in the Jim Crow car

A POEM'S IN HIS HEAD
JUST FOR YOU

For Paul McAllister

Lover
Of Dunbar and corn
Bread poet
Of Lanvale
Street
Row houses
Sunday black
Suits
Grace
Before
Oatmeal
Warm
In canned milk
Simple man
And poet Paul McAllister
Pressed
Pants
For
His friend
A Jew
Men
Stay sharp
Be cool
Pressed
For Jesus
And sudden
Automobile
Death
Crossing

The street
To
The other
Side late
Friday all day
Saturday
Night special
Trouble
Poet Paul black velvet
Skin
Handsome
In himself
Sinner
Done got your
Number
He's writin'
Poems
In his head
Just for you
Mr. Death

THE SHORT UNHAPPY TEEN
YEARS OF DIRTY HARRIET

they tied her to a tree and said
"you are going to like this baby"

spread her on a pool table
chased her down the avenues of

American cities
made sucking noises

and called her "a good fellow"
put a hand on her ass

and winked the good guys
had it coming to

the third date in the backseat of the car
in the living room

they got a squeeze on the couch the
old lady upstairs trying to get some shut-eye

this was a woman's life in Harriet's
factory town drinking

on senior prom losing the cherry
having it busted by a couple guys

good ol' boys ready for college some high
school trim daddy breaking them in

SAM CORNISH

they hang
at the malls "down to the knee caps"

Harriet's sister said "when it comes to a piece
of ass little boys are a chip off the old block"

DIRTY HARRIET*

On Urban Renewal
(*a heroine for Molly Haskell†*)

Dirty Harriet
is not a joke

scumbag

Dirty Harriet
drinks tea

from a small
china cup

Dirty Harriet
has balls

in the palm
of her hand

Dirty Harriet
Don't tell

dirty jokes
scumbag

*Sandra Locke in *Sudden Death,* directed by Clint Eastwood.
†Film critic and feminist.

MONTGOMERY

For Rosa Parks

white woman have you heard
she is too tired to sit in the back
her feet are two hundred years old

move to the back or walk
around to the side door how
long can a woman be a cow

your feet will not move
and you never listen
but even if it rains empty

seats will ride through town
I walk for my children
my feet two hundred years old

SWEET SWEETBACK'S BADASS SONG*

Melvin Van Peebles as Sweetback

Melvin Van Peebles smoking
feets from the city to Mexico

from the North through the West
running black man dogs going for

the legs and dick   sweet
Sweet Sweetback's badass

rippin' through the countryside
in sixties bell-bottoms talking

bright colors runnin' together
an omelette of a man on the run

hair thick as African brush
(you got it) one natural dude

saw the cops   beating a bro' bringing
down the cuffs   then the nightsticks

on his head beaten and beaten
till Sweet Sweetback (Badass)

starts kicking butt breaking
heads until the cops they's

*A film directed, written, and starring Melvin Van Peebles.

dead and set the car afire (something he learned from the Watts

and Detroit Bro's)
that's why he's running

from the cops leaving behind
the ho' houses   the chicks

and pussy the high heels he
walked the floor with the

music that was church to
him Sweetback like an old

sweet song on the road
Sweet Sweetback

is going for the border
no North Star to help   no

church and where is Martin
and Malcolm when a brother

beating on the cops
that whipped some butt "the fight

is on the street" says
Sweet Sweetback bad ass of

the street the fight is on your
feet making tracks looking

back getting Black   Never
looking back

BIGGER THOMAS SAYS SOME BAD
NIGGERS IS OVER THIRTY

Bigger Thomas with a pillow as a weapon
mean enough to turn feathers
into cinder blocks (and that's something
even Jesus can't do)

Bigger Thomas in Cleveland
breaking the heart of Carl Stokes
looking for Malcolm
for Stokely
for H. Rap Brown

Bigger Thomas in Watts
in Detroit
out of work and his mother, his friends,
all the girls on the block,
saying he's lazy

Bigger Thomas cutting up the pool table
pissing in the collection plate
what is that boy worth?
there goes a brick through the
pawnshop window

Bigger
where did you get all those TV sets
(in color too)
Bigger Thomas
scaring his sister
working a rat between his teeth

Bigger Thomas on the roof cleaning
a rifle

"What kind of progress is this?"
asks Edward Brooke

Bigger Thomas
your head is black and just think
you were born sometime around nineteen thirty-nine

I AM MY MOTHER'S DAUGHTER

We burned
Logs

Used charred splinters
For lead

Mashed elderberries I begged
For lamps and broken

Chairs   Sacks for mattresses
Spanish moss for mattress hair

Negro children live
In my heart Africa

Is my blood children breathe
And live I am

My mother's daughter
My life

Is our people
I have prayed in cotton fields

For a small country school
My life is no Africa

My life is our people

Africa is a drum
Beating

In my heart
I am my mother's daughter

Writing
Begging letters

Praying in cotton fields
For a small Negro country school

For I am my mother's
Daughter a drum

Is beating

YOUNG JAMES B.

Young James B. listened to Ma Rainey in Paris, but heard Daddy Sweet
Daddy as a boy. Just a gigolo perhaps, the men at the pulpit, but the
church was their ark against the flood. Church music, safe dance music,
poor man's riches, gin. That little girl, whiskey stabbings, drunks, prosti-
tution, hallways used as toilets. Tuberculosis. Harlem was weary. Eugene
Brown his Holiness, Bishop Sufi Abdul Hameed, AKA the Black Hitler.
The devil's music but Father Divine is Daddy Grace, my own father
thinks they know the fire and brimstone that awaits those who stomp in
the dance hall, women who paint their lips, smoke cigarettes in those
dance halls, speakeasies where you never heard nobody pray. Young James
knows that Daddy's the church. It was a time of great expectations but
the market had just crashed; fell in, others said, long before '29.
There was the other Harlem of Langston, Zora, James Weldon Johnson
and Marcus Garvey, of the Harlem Renaissance. Whites came to listen, to
dance, to sit in the Cotton Club, but then it was over soon and Negroes
were again out of fashion. But James remembers only his father, his mean
stepfather, his mother's children being born, little brothers and sister, and
a schoolteacher bringing a copy of *Uncle Tom's Cabin* for him to read.

THE WORLD OF (SOME OF) OUR
FATHERS

OUR FATHERS

Some of our fathers were quiet men, reading the Afro-American newspapers. They started fires early in the kitchen on cold mornings, lit oil stoves and rolled up newspapers or old magazines, chopped wood for wood stoves in the vacant lot behind the house, and walked each morning to the corner store for the paper. The walk gets longer each year and takes a little longer, and sometimes he sleeps late. When the rooms are warm, we get out of bed, still early, the belly of the wood stove is red and warm, and the house smells of oil and smoky hallways. Some days he just sleeps, although the Depression is over, and drives a taxi or cleans up the movie house, thinking a good job would be in the shipyard. But most of the time he is just thinking. Or fathers on the trains—the B&O traveling from state to state—shining shoes, taking orders, rapping on doors with dinner from the dining car, carrying baggage in some of the best hotels in the country, working the night shift in the post office. Our fathers taught school, ran in the Olympics, wrote the angry novels of the black migrations, the white violence of strikes and the uncertain working day at the shipyards, munitions factories, the hot kitchens of the Navy and Army. In a neighborhood of doctors, lawyers, schoolteachers and bellhops, shoeshine boys, redcaps, porters and men who worked whenever they could, there were men who played cards all day long, and in the evening sang like the Inkspots: "I don't want to set the world on fire . . ."

ALL WE HAVE

Poor white
Why

Did life
Treat
You so

Low
That FDR
Don't
Know

Poor
White
From
Wrong

THEY WON'T FORGET*

she strutted down
the street

in a Georgia town
breasts bouncing

like a movie star
in a sweater

tighter than
a Victorian girdle

and disappeared
into the southern

afternoon they looked
in the basements

of the school
questioned

the Nigger janitor they

said he was sleeping
they dragged the river

asked the Nigger
again they don't

*A 1934 film directed by Michael Curtiz.

SAM CORNISH

believe me
he said to his wife

they'll never
believe me

MEAT

Willie Peterson
Mother believed
He would be president
Someday
Willie Peterson
Ribs cooking
In the electric chair
Willie Peterson
Negro

ELEANOR ROOSEVELT

Ate fried chicken
if necessary
a friend
to the Negro
Franklin Delano Roosevelt
said We Americans
and like the Constitution
meant We White Men
Mrs. Roosevelt believed
there was more
to race
than anti-lynch laws

COUNTRY GATHERS LIKE A SINGLE PERSON

William Randolph Hearst was the first to know that the President was
dead. On the wire in the newsrooms, FDR IS DEAD. Headlines, FDR IS
DEAD. Newsmen fumble in their overcoat pockets, typewriters click,
clack, click, clack . . . . The newsmen are busy putting it down, the war
that Harry Truman had seen take its toll in the face of the President. The
war that was coming to a slow and tragic end. The President wore braces,
and each step, every moment was pain, but the war is still not over.
Death stalked the European countries, the vast oceans and the Asian
world, in Congress, in the White House, everywhere.

Now Truman is notified. NBC interrupts the radio program *Front
Page Farrell* and ABC, *Captain Midnight*. This is where I might have
heard it, on my uncle's radio on McCullough Street, sitting in the living
room, with the flowered paper walls, my mother and aunt in the kitchen
talking, my grandmother a few blocks away, my uncle at work, my friend
Eugene Skates listening to Tom Mix, hearing it on the Mutual Network,
people are on the phone, newsboys take to the streets: Extra, Extra . . .
It is in the long faces on the streets. My Sunday school teacher driving
past the Washington Monument says simply, "Lord." Some of us are
trembling, some of us are afraid. He was like a daddy, a friend.

THE COUNTRY IS DRAPED IN BLACK

Crowds collect in front of the White House. In the morning the
President's body is in his coffin, his lower body covered by his boat cloak,
a flag draped over the casket. Down to the train depot the marchers move
while black accordionist Graham Jackson plays "Going Home," the Negro
spiritual and theme from Dvorak's "New World Symphony." The funeral
train begins its long journey, crowds standing at the crossing collect nearby,
private planes fly overhead. In a cotton field Negro workers bow their
heads and clasp their hands.

Death like the dusk has come: Oh get back, death, but dusk and
death have come way down South. The country seems to gather like a sin-
gle person, trains stop, telephone services are still, radios are silent, subways trains halted, movie theaters, grocery stores shut down, the country
is draped in black. Death like the dusk has come . . . .

ABIDE WITH ME

When the new president Harry S Truman stares at the empty wheelchair, the Navy hymn, "Eternal Father, Strong to Save," a congregation sings . . . my mother calls . . . . When the train passes a man takes off his hat. To the grateful and mourning nation, his death is as important and moving as Abraham Lincoln's. He died in the White House: a soldier at attention. The parade moves along the avenue, from Union Station toward the Capitol, the drums beat, the honor guard stands, the war continues. He brought us out of the Depression into war, a soldier thinks, a long time ago, it seems. He recalls the soup lines, the dust storms, the black clouds, the dry brown lands, the dry years of Prohibition. The infantry mourns Roosevelt as they hunt Japs and in anger remember Pearl Harbor, the empty factories and stores and the jobs that were not there. Thousands of Japs were killed and thousands more captured and still the war continued. The soldiers, sailors, marines, will miss Roosevelt. It was like he was always there.

And he was a friend to the Negro. A. Philip Randolph, and Mary McLeod Bethune, all friends and advisors of Eleanor Roosevelt . . . as the country lost Lincoln so today we lose Roosevelt, black Americans and white Americans gather in the White House.

The body of the President rides through the night, the President's body is watched and remembered by an old Negro couple. The words fall upon the streets of New York shouted by newsboys written in lights in Times Square, in buses, in the subways. In the windows of the shops, from Saks to corner stores, the pictures of the President hang. Fast falls the evening tide. The darkness deepens. Lord, with me abide or, as the song goes, I am feeling down. I am feeling blue. Americans face the radios like a picture was before them. Memorial buttons sell for fifteen cents. My mother and grandmother look strangely at me. Washington (where the Bonus Army fled) is nearby.

We hear the newsboys in the streets below. There are people in this state who remember Roosevelt as a boy, others as a young man in Hyde Park, the town cop says. Long after the crowds and the train departed:

"He's gone."

"I never heard of a president like you," a letter writer once wrote, but it was Eleanor who was his legs and his presence in the ghettos, the cotton fields, the churches, and schools. Eleanor in a long black coat. When she died it was said by Adlai Stevenson that a light had gone out of the world. "Unnumbered centuries are hers," a line I recall from a poem by James Weldon Johnson.

HIROSHIMA MY LOVE

Based on the film by Alan Renais

they are a landscape   in dust a sweat
moving
he is   Hiroshima black rain   they are lovers
a city   a sun   this fire "I was there," he said
"no" she replies   her arms tighten   he slips
in them   she is Paris   he is Hiroshima
he is a city   she is a woman   "I saw the sun
turn
to ash that fell and the children . . . my amour
my Hiroshima"

HOGMEAT

SOME CHITTERLINGS FOR JOE

Joe Louis
A credit to his race
In the ring
was mean as a town where a Negro could
Not let the sun set
on him
Mean as a Texas sun
The brown bomber stepped
Into the ring
In the shacks
In the tenements he made his people
(down and out) holler
Like a blues song
the brown bomber
knocked
them white boys out
A dusk song for the brown bomber
How 'bout some chitterlin's
For Joe (they stink worse than feets)
But they's good eatin'
Some hog meat for Joe   made real
Fine

STRONG

For Sterling Brown*

Poet
Man
Reading
Strong
Black
Man
Reading
Could have been
A white
Man
In town
A Joel
Chandler
Harris Negro
Instead
Of a low-
Down blues
Poet
Throwing
A few licks
Like a darkie
In a honky
Tonk
Strong men
Keep on
Coming
Said Sterling
Deep

*An African American poet of the 1930s.

Voice
Sterling
Listen
To his music
The voice
Of
Sterling
Brown
Man
Reading

THE GREEN HORNET*

For James and Matt at Comicopia

Green Hornet in his green mask overcoat pants and brown shoes   from
          a long line of masked men   mysterious men
hard jaws   blue eyes   and iron blooded friends of the people
          the workers   downtrodden
by the banks   the ruthless government   the John Dillingers and bad
Pretty Boy Floyds Al Capones   The Green Hornet with his Chinese
chauffeur (friend & companion) butt kicking   arm twisting
          neck breaking   chopping   Kato "broke your fuckin' back"
          sidekick Kato
in black uniform long dark polished nails
detests Indian and Jap Greaser sidekicks
Green Hornet "got no time" for shivering knee knocking Negro chauffeur
          Mantan Moreland

Green Hornet   Yankee "smash yo' face" cleaning house
hits the streets   on two wheels
Hornet's car buzz like a bee
his gas gun puts men to sleep
zips through the night
like a firefighter
a cop

Green Avenger
defender of the weak and despised   save the night
give us the day
deliver us
the law into your green gloved hands

*1940s comic book hero created by Fran Striker.

Green Hornet
AKA blonde blue-eyed playboy in your mansion
cave like the Dark
Knight of Gotham City
green raincoat and narrow brim hat
green leather gloves to protect
your fists   (well manicured nails for dinners and the ladies) ready
to break the jaw the arms
of Wop Bootleggers Nigger Numbermen   Chinamen   Warriors
Pimps

Street Walkers   Lawyers Pawnbrokers and Crooked Cops
preying upon the weak hiding behind the courts
the judges
and lawyers laughing at justice
priest and altar boys

give them
The sting
of The Greeeeeen Hornet
zzzz zzzz zzzz zzzz zzzz zzzz zzzz zzzz zzz

SAM CORNISH

THE CLEAN WELL DRESSED MEN*

in this Midwestern town
you don't wear suits and high

shined shoes   in a diner
night never falls   but comes

with the changing of menu
raising the prices dinner

is a few more bucks   old
men linger over their peas

the mashed are brown
with gravy and run

with butter the coffee
is a few hours old

and still good the Nigger
is good in the kitchen

and someone always asks
where does he live

where does he go when
the diner shuts down

and he sits down with
the old man and the boy

*A 1946 film noir based on the Hemingway story "The Killers" directed by
Robert Siodmak.

104

and has a bite but tonight
that will not happen   these

men are in town and not
for steak or chicken

the peas and mashed
they want something to drink

and all the diner serves is
Seven Up and tea coffee

or milk and the steam tables
(the food is great here)

are not up   but the streets
are emptying the bars are

acting up   the smell of supper
drifts down from the houses

along the back streets and
the lamplights come on

and there is dusk   three
strange white men in

a town with one movie house
a church a school that has

one room and old maid
schoolteacher a gas station

at the edge at the edge of town

THE PHANTOM LADY*

Night after cold night she is here
the dark haired white woman

they call phantom lady
having a drink lighting up like a movie star

her cigarette (just a prop)
she thinks she is Joan Crawford

once a hard woman of pots and pans
a life in dishwater

her fingernails worn and working
at the typewriter

high above the city she is a workhorse
set free from the kitchens

by the war
to sit and smoke watching men

day in day out waiting all night
for something young and tight he thinks

(like me) but she sits   not young
enough for a pickup

bartender the phantom
lady waits for you

*A film noir directed by Robert Siodmak.

BOOGIE WOOGIE

When every bar
Downtown
Is named
The Bucket
Of Blood
Dizz and Louie
's cutting up
Girl
Ain't you
Glad you are
Brown
and fine

JACKIE ROBINSON

the uniform and ball
are white but Jackie is

New Jersey
Harlem   separate drinking fountains
empty seats
at the back
of a southern bus
my world is on fire
my world is Sunday
and someday
Jackie in his uniform
white enough to be America

but now Jackie shines
like Louis Armstrong
like a preacher
in the church
he's the rock
the hidin' place
the uniform and the ball
and Jackie Robinson Negro

MISTER

For Daddy King

our preacher
stood up

a Moses
for his people

white men called
him Mister

to his face
boy

to his back
nigger

in their
dreams

he was my father
in the pulpit

he was God
to me

they put his
name on

our church

white men
called him "Mr"

LADY DAY

black don't crack
but

Billie did
Lady Day

big woman
all that misery

is a song
the band helps

out
a little

but them that's got
the Bible says

"is them that has"
Billie

is on her own
some other girls

stole her tunes
soundin'

like Billie
takes the money

out of
her pocketbook

black
don't crack

just gets
hungry

fades
like Billie did

SUCKED HIS DICK
CUT HIS THROAT

Poor women
Were his
Crime
They kneeled
Before
Sparklin'
Teeth
He loved all
Colors
But burned
His head
With Dixie Peach

LISTEN TO THE MEN LIKE
GLORIA DID

For Gloria Naylor

daybreak in Brewster Place
listen to heartache

in Brewster Place   Negro
men from the darkest place

the deep deep South from land
to factories   slopping

floors   at noon sometimes
they rest with a little taste

quiet men troubled all Brewster's
God from preacher man God's man

Gloria tells us how they
live that way slaving

janitor schoolhouse
jazz man livin'   their whiskey

playin' out   that man loves
men   like I love my gin

life is like a spittoon
expectin' big things

daytime in Brewster Place
listen to the men like Gloria did

SAM CORNISH

WHERE THE DAYTIME FALLS

Sinatra and Armstrong
together swinging in the street

from every Negro window
Louie with the smile and sweat

Frankie the crooner the mobster
together in the wee small hours

the moon is still
the city is just about to wake up

the world is stretching out
the milkman   the early morning

radio   the cop checks the doors
of the pawn shops the back streets

the downtown and waterfront
is the smell of coffee and bacon

the diners and greasy spoons
open to say "good morning"

the entire city is in the voice
of two men

Louis's wonderful world
Frank's wee small hours

WHAT I DON'T HAVE IN SPADES

they were called Dream Girls
were gum chewing sisters
poppin' fingers
and stuff

the torch and blues songs
are gone
like the streets
the bars and the smoky rooms
where I danced
out the weekend
into the next
day thinking
"this is soul"
that's what those Dream Girls got
with their big hair
and eye makeup

those sisters
should be in church
up the street
instead of coming out of the jukebox
off the record players
on stage
doing their silly little steps
that have the boys
saying "cool"
the girls thinking "they ain't so hot
what's Miss Ross got
that I don't have in spades"

SOUTHLAND

Ray Charles
is an old

sweet
song

on my mind
Ray Charles

singing
all night

long
singing

sweetly this
song

the whole night
through

Georgia
Georgia

CARMEN JONES*

Dorothy Dandridge

is fire and teasing
brown

full of sun
and mystery

hips churning
in your face

with a razor
in her stockings

no scrubbing floors
for Negro men

or white
her life

is in her hips
Carmen's mouth is painted

red
but sun and God

have made her
brown

*A 1954 film directed by Otto Preminger.

not afraid of sin
or the South

fuck Mississippi
and the Klan

life is short
and morning

(in colored town)
comes too soon

WE HAVE NEVER LOVED

we have
never
loved
each other
we
have
only
this house
this street
these neighborhoods
to misunderstand
ourselves
this food
these wages
it is
not love
but
something
deeper
than fear
that makes
you call me
brother
in a strange
city
of white
men

MAMA MINE

For Hattie McDaniel

Mama's childr'n
sittin' at her knee

White children
listen   Mama's

songs solid as a tree
Colored children

think Mama
thank God

Black ain't white
God done left you

the light
Al Jolson "Your Mama

Mine" no minstrel's song
you ever work your

mother so hard
like my Mama Mama

mine

NEGRO WOMEN OF THE MOVIES*

Negro women   yesterday's Black woman   living the cops say on
          Tobacco Road
proud and loud "moving on up"   long gone those misery days   life is
          a ladder
and "I am ready to climb" with you and sorrow in one mouth
movie mother Miss Blues Auntie and Jesus to a nation
blues don't make her weep   trouble come and I see trouble go
brown work and skin is not a tragic tale and banana yellow peach light
          might be passin' and plenty of lips for lovin' servants to the
          world hallelujah soul savin' Sunday backslidin' weekdays when the
          dining room doors flung open and she came in like dawn breakin'
takin' on work like Jesus to the crown   Aunt Sue with Langston's stories
          (and poems)
tired beautiful smile buckwheat lady on the pancake box
hungry "come around the back door honey"
kept the country going and always behavin'
Hattie McDaniel
Louise Beavers
Miss Beavers Miss McDaniel to you   these is churchgoin' ladies
on the weekend slavin' up a storm
white people wanted her in the kitchen
(not heaven nor the bus and theater) smelling
like soap stale bed sheets and baked bread
a colored woman always
polite openin' doors   fresh crisp white collar crisp 'round
her neck fingers workin'
nightfall women they were women of Madison and Druid Hill Avenues
and boiling teas sittin' back and liftin' their feet from the floor
put back their heads and sighed and began

*Louise Beavers in *Imitation of Life* (dir. John Stahl, 1934) and Hattie McDaniel in
Gone With the Wind (dir. Victor Fleming, 1939).

to talk about working
for white folks' children
that grow up
someday and go far
away daughters who marry and stay close
fresh grandchildren sweet as water

COFFIN AND DIGGER

For Chester Himes and his Harlem crime novels

their faces cut up
backs out of shape

loving black pussy
Billie Holiday's

lips to suck on
the cops

of Chester Himes
are Negro

cops nasty
as White men

on chain gangs
meaner than Jack

O Diamonds
ripping

through the streets
guns blazing

crazy Niggers
diggin' over

golden brown
peach skin

apricot brown
chippies

lovin' cabarets
Chester Himes'

Harlem cops
are kicking ass

I'd better stick
with the white boys

Coffin Ed and Digger
Jones

STREET SONG

Freedom train
Freedom train
Ride here

On the
Avenue
Just my bottle and me

FRANKIE HAS A SONG FOR YOU

SINATRA

For the Honorable Thomas M. Menino,
Mayor of Boston

in the late hours
of Saturday night

at the end
of the week

in every corner
of my room

Frankie has
a song for me

in the low
breaking dawn

the endless
Fifth Avenue

of my memory
the voice

is Sinatra
he is a song

that follows me
through the lonely

city nights
and smoke-

filled bars
of drink after

drink and lighting
up letting

the smoke rise
into the air

drop a nickel
in the machine

Frankie has
a song for you

PICKUP ON SOUTH STREET*

I. Working Woman

—Jean Peters as Candy

Candy is working the "Johns" in the back rooms off the avenues
she is a swift walking piece of hard talking womanhood
working the streets overtime a Catholic girl of the boulevard
she stuffs the poor box and sits in the dark confessing
to the priest "I have sinned" and he nods to the blow jobs
says "mercy" to the hand jobs the straight quick fucking
she is a working girl "and this father" she says "is my job"
Candy genuflects before Christ Mary Mother of Jesus
forgives the cops on the beat heads between
her legs getting a free one whispering
"is this good for you Baby"

II. A Kiss in Your Pocket

—Richard Widmark as Skip McCoy

find Skip McCoy hustling suckers in department stores   the subway
young couples tightly holding on to one another
drifting through life among their unbearable children
fire engines and stuffed rabbits toys of his youth
tobacco his father smelled of after supper
think of Skip as a man so deep into his newspaper
you feel the *The New York Times* is hitting on him

*A film written and directed by Sam Fuller, 1953. From a story by Dwight Taylor.

131

with panty and girdle ads and liberal editorials
news of street crimes in Harlem and the Bowery
or is he just a businessman keeping up with Wall Street
and the people of New York
Skip McCoy pickpocket   smooth cannon
at your service and his own
His hands are in your pockets   hip and overcoat
close to your heart and buttocks
lifting wallets so gently you sigh
he is working the streets and subways

like a hobby taking change and bills
from stiffs in crowds   at fires evictions
in holiday shopping malls   Radio
City   In Grand Central Station he stands so close
to you it is a flirtation   a kiss in your pocket
a hand upon the heart and elbow
"excuse me" and opening a door
saying "thank you"
to himself
he is a lowlife of the streets
a hard working man of the city
dressed as fine as you please

III. Promise

—*Thelma Ritter as Moe*

Moe the old lady sells ugly neckties   on side streets
main drags   collects Rudy Vallee records
loves Bing Crosby doing "Pennies from Heaven"
his cross-eyed cool singing "for you and me"
voice so sweet and distant
the night is a promise

singing to her each night
in her room
from her record player
she stares at the turntable
listens to the 78s
and beneath it all she knows
that someone is waiting for her

TAXI DRIVER*

Mr. Law and Order
Mr. Crime in the streets

He's the Vet ducking
behind tables and chairs

in your living room   smoking
grass   taking no prisoners

he's Travis taxi driver   (fare
even to Harlem)   he's cool

gun belts hold up his pants
mohawk hair cut down

the center of his head   bad
(and that ain't good Nigger

boy) he checks out
7-Eleven   Little Peach

White Hen Pantrys   Korean
Liquor stores with a sawed off

shotgun   wired up
on Oliver Stone

movies and Martin Scorsese hood
(no Spike Lee neo-black Nationalism)

*A film directed by Martin Scorsese starring Robert De Niro.

he goes to Harlem   likes pretty browns
nightclubs that wail   armed to kill

pimps of all colors
Travis cut your pony tail ass

"just like a Nigger" says Travis
"to come in a chick's face"

(it's okay man she'll   let
you)   Travis talks

to mirrors wants to know if his
image is checking him out

(how cool when you ask yourself
"you looking at me"

and draw   point a finger and shoot
double-jointed thumb like a hammer

click)   in his cab he listens to jazz and
filmscores on the tape

Herrmann and Goldsmith (music teachers
adopt this boy)

"listen to me are you listening to me"
Travis talks with his music   others merrily sing

MARS ATTACKS*

Mars attacks   Loews Sony Theaters   Drive Ins   shopping malls
old churches and supermarket marquees and comic book
stores   bad movies   in the dark they were ashamed
treated like Butterfly McQueen
Mars Attacks   network TV
White women in aprons sitting at tables serving frozen food dinners
watching the *Twilight Zone* Rod Serling's Martians say "llawethtaniagapu"
Mars attacks Black people AKA Negroes/Colored/African/American/Niggers
bus tore up Washington, DC, looks like 60s riot Green men shootin'
up like addicts   Martians rippin' sides of tenements shootin' the president
and his skinny wife   "hctibnikcuf" Mars attacks pork chops polyester
black movies   Booty Call *Superfly* (now they goin' too far) educated bloods
say "cool" big teeth motherfuckers "paaaaaaazzpaz"   we talk shit too go up
"elohssae" the sky is falling   Martians hanging together "ganbganbganb" cool
green fire melts cement   the front steps old ladies & hippies take
to the mountains like Indians with vegetables   wait for tomorrow
but Big Jim Brown Pharaoh Brown fists like boulders pounds little
green men to jelly wins back America one little green son of a bitch at a time
Fish stores   Chinese Take-out   Rib Joints   dogs and CNN talking heads
Niggers on street   hophead shootin' stuff Martians talk "emacuoypish
ethdnanamtaruoy kcuf" Mars attacks trailer camps   America's Heartland
"kecndersrekecuf eeheeheeh" down come the faces
of the Founding Fathers (where are the mothers)
Little Green Men chewing gum
Pharaoh Big Jim Brown comin' to whip yo' little green ass   "Watch the streets
watch the streets"

*A film by Tim Burton, which is a satire on the science fiction of H. G. Wells and the
black exploitation cinema of the 1970s.

THOUSANDS MAKE THE DUSK OF AFRICA

SWEET SONG

ONCE IN ALL THE WORLD

Now in the long night someone is lighting a candle in a room far away
from the freeway, in a house that sits close to the side of a forgotten road
where the schoolhouse is. Still one room and the same grim people waiting for the world to be set afire and the four horsemen riding through the
clouds of morning. I think of the green trees of my youth, cats that slept
on porches, the sight of chicken on the chopping block, the thump of my
father's axe, and the look on my mother's face. Those awful days were not
the same as the misery days of my grandparents, when women were
named Moses and saw the burning bush, heard in the mountains the sudden rush, the breath of the wind which is voice on the mountain, when
the lives of the Jews in bondage were the fires burning angrily in the
bosom of my people, my family. There was a deep hunger somewhere in
those days which I began to feel when women were washed free of sin in
the creek, and the men walked into the cold water, dipped and baptized
in its purity. They came to the pulpit and passed out, woke hollering His
Blessed Name. The women had more children than the old woman who
lived in a shoe; lice crawled through their hair, and the comb was hard on
the scalp. They ate from a bowl in the center of the floor and my mother
fed us from the scraps hidden in her apron and brought home.

THE SOUTH WAS WAITING

In Baltimore Ruth Brown sang bad
Songs about her brown
Body but I saw white boys hit
The nigger
Streets looking for colored
Girls
The fifties
Were marches
Integrating
Schools young
Richard Nixon
Barbers standing
In the stores
Of barbershops yelling
Shame
Shame
At the sight
Of my hair
Negro men
conked
Their hair to make
It good
Like singer Nat
King Cole
Emmett Till died
In Mississippi
His picture
In *JET*
Magazine
His death a word
On the streets I never
Marched in Mississippi

Taught in freedom
Schools signed Negro
Men and women
To vote
During the bus boycotts
Nor sat in for
Civil rights
And hamburgers
I was poor even
Then my shoes were holes
Held together by threats
And good luck
But I read Camus and listened
to Martin Luther King, Jr.

the Muslims
in the temple selling
bean pie
and promising the death of
the white man
I read about Algeria and found
James Baldwin
Disturbing (but
Didn't know why)
Some of my friends
Joked about
Sippi yes I didn't
Ride the freedom bus
But I walked
The streets
Of Baltimore
Visited
Little Italy
The Polish
Neighbors

Near the waterfront
You didn't have
To ride
To the southern states
It was waiting
In Baltimore

THE RIVER THE WORLD KNOWS

I knew the boy
I saw the flat nose
Those thick lips and dark skin
So black for a northern boy
And now even darker 'cause of the sun
And Deep South
And then I saw his ring
And I knew that this was my nephew
Pulled from the river like so
so many others thrown into the river
and now dead
for the Negro to see

SAM CORNISH

MY LORD WHAT A MORNING

Negroes dug into their pockets
For his mother   gathered
Their pennies   dressed
In their Sunday clothes
My mother hand-washed my shirt
Ironed my pants shined
My shoes with liquid wax
We walked to church we stood
In line to see
The corpse of Emmett Till

FANNIE LOU HAMER

Fannie
Lou
Hamer
Unknown
In Chicago
Classrooms
Was
Appreciated
Elsewhere
For
Her
Big
Black
Mouth
In the
South
Fannie
Lou
Ate
Her
Greens
Tended
Her
Land
And wanted
To
Vote

Negro
Men
Were found
At the bottom

Of the river
For wanting
Less
But
Fannie
Marched
To the courthouse
Big
As a fist
Black
As the ground
Underfoot

FREEDOM SCHOOL

Children at recess thinking
Of Marcus Garvey
in some imperfect
Song
hold our hands
we are their teachers
In our classrooms
we say black
Is a color
black is me
we love you
Black brothers
and sisters
Our people
Home in Africa

BUS BOYCOTT

We
Come home
Ready to fight
The waitress
The short-order cooks
The counters
And stools with brown bags
Served at the take-
Out window
Came
To a white South
That said
No to Mrs. Parks
Whose feet
Said enough

THE VERTICAL NEGRO
TO MR. JIM CROW

At the Woolworth's
Lunch counter

What a shame
It is America

To be
And salute standing

Up sitting
Down to be America`

LUNCH

At first we thought
All neat brushed shined
And tired America sat
With us marched
Stood with us
Waiting
For a cup of coffee
America with a fresh
Washed face
Polite
Patient America
Churchgoing America
Saying no more
Back door
And Howard Johnson
Take-out
Have a seat
Sit down
Langston Hughes
Darker
Brother you have
Waited
So long

TIRED FROM WALKING BUT NOT TIRED ENOUGH
TO SIT DOWN IN THAT BUS

They bombed Dr. King's house and we kept on a comin'
Like the Sterling Brown's strong men

They put Miss Parks in handcuffs
A nice respectable colored woman

In jail and we started walking
Kept on walking until our feet gave way
But we walked
The church was set afire our songs
No longer sorrow songs

But the words that once kept us going
Like we did Harriet following

The North Star through the woods
Kept on walking

On all kinds of tired feet flat feet
Feet that shouted

When they sank into the warm water
Brought from the stove

And poured into the washbasin
Even in church we were tired

But not tired
Enough to sing leaning

On the everlasting arm

THAT KIND OF PREACHING

When I heard the boycott
Was over I could not keep

From crying I should have
Sung a hymn but I am

Not that kind
Of a man

JAMES BALDWIN

Fire in the city   and Malcolm
has no pity   Bigger Thomas   this
is the threshing floor meet
your terrible maker   Uncle Tom
spent and wasted father burnt
out like a Harlem full of anger
fire make me a world this time

MY BROTHER IS HOMEMADE

My brother is homemade
Like he is the first real
Black boy I ever knew
Before Richard Wright
And Baldwin
Found black summers
In Harlem and Mississippi
He taught me how
To drink at age five
And a half
He cleaned the streets
With bullies
And stolen ice cream
He came into this color
Thing lighter than me
Yellow and shiny dark hair
But to make a point
Grew blacker than most

THINGS OF THE STREET

Today my brother is leaving home. He will not be leaving the neighbor-hood but just leaving us, not saying where he is going or why he is leav-ing the three rooms where we have lived together as a family for so many years. Brothers are things of winter and summer, of long legs and growing up, walking down the aisle on Sunday morning, a man ready to take the body of the Lord into his mouth, to drink the Welch's Grape Juice of the Lord, in long pants yet. Brothers are moments always waiting to be, standing in the shadows of condemned buildings, baseball glove in hand, comic book in back pockets and schoolbooks on the ground ready to slide home. Or, like Jackie Robinson, to steal home. The street where the bad Lance boys, or even the Badger boys that have been in junior high are ready to ask for dues or are first with swipes upon my bald head, my brother is the neighborhood Brown Bomber . . . . Ah brother, pushing a baby carriage through the street like a peddler with a cart. Brothers are also things of the streets when everything is wrong. My brother when I was afraid of brown dogs with long paws, dogs barking, galloping dogs, watchdogs, dogs that charged the fences and pounded upon the gates, tugged at the leash, and barked all night, stray dogs, pet dogs, dogs in my sleep, plunging into the darkness, digging bones from the earth, dogs that smell like streets and backyards, dogs that smell of fried fish and horse stables and hay where horses shit, and streets where policemen rode, hands boldly on their hips, red-faced and mean as the dogs that snapped at the air as I passed them on the way to school. Dogs that lunged at demonstrators in Selma, in Birmingham, at lunch counters and marches. Dogs that worked for the deep South and barked, Never! Never! Never!

BIRMINGHAM 1968

They were just
four

little girls
in a church

not old
enough

to know
the Lord

forgave them
for being

born

four

little girls
ribbons

in their greased
tight hair

DEATH OF DR. KING

We sat outside
the bars
The dime stores
Everything is closed today
We are mourning
Our hands are full
With bricks
A brother died today
My eyes are wet
Water is in my hands
This is grief

BROTHER POET

For Roger Tazwell, hero of any street

A brother with a strut shot
Down in his prime   bad
Poet of the nasty street poet called the living
Lips

RAY CHARLES

do you
dig ray
charles

when the
blues are
silent

in his throat

& he rolls
up his
sleeves

LONG HAIR THANK GOD
ALMIGHTY NAPPY HAIR

With a hundred curls
Upon my head

Thousands make the dusk
Of Africa

There
God gave me

And some of us
This hair forever

Nappy and long

BLACK POET NEGRO NO MORE

That's me a nigger
poet
set free a poem a black poem
a criminal white haired (the only thing white
about me) dirty old man
that's me Georgia
I am looking for work
no gambling or nightlife
just women yellow brown black redbone
that's me a black
man poetry set free

1976

some of us will go
to Africa
to Mecca
to the third world
to basements with wire
and the little red book
strange white women
with credit cards
some of us will give
our nickels and dimes
to the church
buy we hope small
pieces of God
others will kill the women
who marry the men
of God some of us
will kill
the word

FOR BEING THERE

they dragged him on the back
roads of a Texas town

with his blood on their shoes
they were singing "Deep

in the Heart of Texas
the Stars Are Bright"

this Texas Negro hauled
over gravel and stones

the dust of a little town
in Texas for being there

SAM CORNISH

BOOM BOX*

For Jerry Barrax

Boom Box
swaying

out the projects
big black kid

putting Public Enemy
on the street

loud

in his head
is getting

on the nerves cops
with fingers

in their ears
people running

out of the pizza
shop

not waiting
for the onions

the anchovies
getting

*A character in Spike Lee's film *Do the Right Thing.*

too much tomato
Boom Box

is HERE big

loud MOTHER FUCKER
with a radio

on his shoulder
no brains

just RAPPIN'

shit
going in one ear

Public Enemy
doing his thing

girls say
going in his head

and staying
there

Boom Box
shakes

the sidewalks
the house

the entire summer
Boom Box

SAM CORNISH

Detroit and Watts
burn baby

in his head
he makes Negro

music an angry sound
no Michael Jackson

or Supremes in Boom Box
just a lot

of pissed off music
getting

down on you BEATING
you makin'

you mad enough
to KILL

SOLDIER'S STORY*

Glen Thurman as C.J. †

ask him a question he'll
sing you a song   C.J. picking

guitar hang your head
like a heavy load   C.J. is

the blues he sings
walking   mean Nigger trouble

on the street corner head busting
Saturday night   C.J.

is chitterlin'-watermelon-eating-
guitar-playing nigger

Texas dusty towns and juke
joints   church clapping Jesus

& Sunday morning in the Bottom
lands C.J. a Buck   shot

full of whiskey   white men like him
name him Shine call   him

Coon   Burr Head Boy Hoss
Liver lips   Jig   Jigaboo Dinge

C.J. Just grins   and shines

* Negro soldier in the play and film, *Soldier's Story*.
†The actor in the Norman Jewison film of the same name.

THE SOUTH IS MY HOME

—Spanning the 1960s, from the civil rights era to Black Power

Because God wrote that book instead of Harriet Beecher Stowe
Because Uncle Tom is dead
Because the KKK rides to the rescue in *Birth of a Nation*
Because Jim Crow is not a Disney character
Because the Negro cannot read
Because the blues is a white man's song the Negro lives everyday
Because Elvis is the only nigger allowed in the American living room
Because some of you are bored
Because some of you read only Jane Austen
Because thousands and thousands are coming to Mississippi this summer
Because many thousands are gone
Because of Amos and Andy
Because my father is a Democrat
Because my mother is a Republican
Because I feel the weekend in my feet
Because the South is in my blood I am waiting for the prophet Elijah
Because I am one of Abraham's children
Because of *Gone With the Wind*
Because there is no promised land
Because *Gone With the Wind* is another book cutting down trees
Because *Life* is a magazine
Because *Look* magazine has not looked at Mississippi
Because *Ebony* magazine sells skin lightener to Negroes using light-
        skinned models
Because there is no skin cream to make you black
Because I am the son of Ham and my father was in his cups
Because John Howard Griffin wrote a book entitled *Black Like Me*
Because Jesus was here and gone
        and never stopped for my pot liquor hamhocks and read E.
        Franklin Frazier

Because I am Bigger Thomas
Because some of you read Shakespeare and nothing else
Because Allen Ginsberg said fuck you America
Because I am going to vote
Because I can't read the whites-only sign
Because I am a boy sixty-three years old
Because I know the Mississippi is a river named Emmett Till
Because Rosa Parks is a paper bag brown and still can't sit down
Because my name is one line crossin' over 'nother
Because Uncle Tom is not dead
Because I can't spell Negro
Because Watts is burning
Because the great books are not the only books
Because the South must handle its own problems
Because young students are marching
Because the young Negroes have washed and cut their hair have parted
        their short hair
and it is fresh and gray
Because like morning their faces shine with pride like dusk
Because they are wearing new suits and dresses and full of pride and fear
        and sit trembling
Because they sit at the Woolworth's counters and wanted
not the cup of coffee they asked for the menu or anything on it but to sit
        down in America
I am marching because they are sitting and waiting for America to stand
        up with them
Because I am singing "Lift Every Voice and Sing"
Because this is a new day they are thinking we shall overcome
Because you whip a Negro like a woman
Because Negroes are men and women boys and girls
Because Emmett Till is a Negro boy
Because the South is my home
Because you are an asshole

EPILOGUE

ELEGY

My father knew we were afraid and he was also afraid so that night after
dinner, he brought a chair from the kitchen, put a shotgun across his lap
and rocked back and forth & was cold because the sun went down early
and the blackness of the woods around us made the world seem still and I
felt like a young boy that everything was going to last forever because my
father was outside our house ready to fight to protect myself, my mother
and younger brother. I have wondered why I have not heard much about
men like my father instead of those songs that sing why do you treat me
so . . . my father was not a good man seldom home and mean to my
mother and short-tempered with his sons. But he was that night the
father I remembered sitting on the porch because he heard a Negro had
talked back to some white man in town.

A PERSONAL GLOSSARY
OF THE SIGNIFICANCE OF THE
FOLLOWING REFERENCES

Abdul Hamid, Sufi (b. Eugene Brown, aka Bishop Amiru al Munimin)—1930s convert to Islam and creator of the Harlem Jobs in the Community Campaign. His detractors claimed that boycotted businesses were forced to hire African Americans or pay protection money, leading to his nickname, "The Black Hitler."

Baldwin, James—African American writer who broke from the Naturalism established by Richard Wright with his essays and portrayal of homosexuality in American life.

Beavers, Louise—On a personal note, because she resembled my mother, a dominant heavyset woman who was always in control regardless of her roles as a servant in American films and who said she'd rather "play a maid than be a maid."

Bethune, Mary McLeod—Negro educator who founded a school for African-American children and worked in the Roosevelt Administration, was a friend and supporter of Eleanor Roosevelt.

Brooke, Edward—A role model for me, a sophisticated Republican and an ideal example of "compassionate conservatism."

Brown, H. Rap—Bigmouthed and mean-spirited spokesman for the student nonviolent committee in the 1960s. When H. Rap Brown spoke, cities burned.

Brown, John—An Abolitionist was so opposed to slavery, he declared war on that peculiar institution at Harpers Ferry. He was hanged for his beliefs.

Brown, Ruth—Husky-voiced soul singer in my youth who made famous the song "Fine brown frame. I wonder what could be his name?"

Brown, Sterling—Almost white but black, dialect poet with a strong feeling for Negro folklore and the voice of the rural South. A militant descendant of the Paul Laurence Dunbar school.

Carmichael, Stokley—Articulate, always in a suit but another burner of cities and disparaging of the Old Negro School, the NAACP and all Negroes.

Dandridge, Dorothy—Actress, Academy Award nominee and tragic figure of the American cinema.

Divine, Father—A charismatic opportunist and man of God and the community who both exploited and gave dignity and inspiration to the Negro people of his time.

Douglass, Frederick—Former slave, abolitionist and feminist, national and world leader and author of the classic book on slavery, *The Narrative of the Life of Frederick Douglass*, An American Slave, who taught himself to read. An amazing man.

Dunbar, Paul Laurence—Major poet of the nineteenth century, both a formal lyric and dialect poet and writer of fiction.

Garvey, Marcus—Just as a note of interest, think of any current-day male political leader who would name a ship, as he did, after an American woman poet? Father of the "Back to Africa" movement and of twentieth century black consciousness and separatism.

Hamer, Fannie Lou—Prominent civil rights leader of the 1960s. She was not well educated but she was a well-spoken, forceful woman.

Harris, Joel Chandler—Southern white man who created Uncle Remus, a character that may be one of the early examples of Negro folklore recorded by a white man—patronizing but nonetheless an invaluable view of white-on-black relations.

Hart, Philip—An actual slave. Little else is known about him.

Himes, Chester—Began his writing career highly influenced by Richard Wright but as an expatriate living in Paris, created a series of Harlem crime novels that reflected the influences of the pulp novel in America at its very best.

Holiday (Lady Day), Billie—Through her voice she exemplified what an artist can do through oral interpretation. She imposed her own life on songs that were often created by white composers.

Hughes, Langston—Most prolific black writer of the twentieth century, poet, essayist, short story writer. He captured the daily life of the American Negro. His language and speech patterns, sense of hope and religious beliefs. For me, he was the Negro Whitman.

Hurston, Zora Neale—A Negro woman writer with a strong appeal to white readers for her narrow focus without any social content or commentary on post–Civil War and segregated America by telling charming, sometimes vivid feminist tales that never reflected the social injustices of her time.

Jim Crow—The post–Civil War segregation laws separating blacks and whites and legalizing a separate but unequal America.

Johnson, James Weldon—The gentleman of the Negro poems, pre–Harlem Renaissance, famous for his novel, The *Autobiography of an Ex-Coloured Man*, a novel about passing for white. In considerable detail, it details the options available to a Negro man of education: either pass for white or take menial jobs, etc., and the possibilities of lynching.

Johnson, Robert—Perhaps the most famous and legendary blues singer. Rumor has it that his was not so much a talent but an ability acquired by a bargain struck with the devil (as exemplified in the film *Brother, Where Art Thou?*).

Jolson, Al—Jazz singer who starred in one of the first talking picture by that title and performed in blackface Stephen Foster songs about the old Negro who learned his lesson in the North and returned to the South where whites loved and understood him and he, of course, found his place.

Kemble, Fanny—Along with Harriet Beecher Stowe, one of the first writers of antislavery and abolitionist literature. Actress and aunt of Owen Wister (author of *The Virginian*) and all-around influential and provocative woman of the nineteenth century. Fanny did it all.

King, Daddy—Father of Martin Luther King, Jr., and perhaps a stronger and more militant figure in a segregated era and not necessarily a student of nonviolence. He was uppity.

Louis, Joe—Heavyweight champion of the 1930s and 1940s, all-around role model and acknowledged "credit to his race."

McDaniel, Hattie—Academy Award–winning actress for *Gone With the Wind*. A comedian and portrayer of strong-willed, sassy Negro slaves and domestics.

Mix, Tom—Cowboy actor in the movies, comic books, and on radio. Had a Negro sidekick named Wash who referred to him as "Mr. Tom."

Naylor, Gloria—Feminist and contemporary African-American woman writer best known for her novels *The Women of Brewster Place*, *Mama Day*, and *Linden Hills*. With the possible exception of Gayl Jones, perhaps the best African American woman writer of her generation. Few can equal her in her portraits of African American men in relation to women and to each other.

Peterson, Willie—Fictional character, a composite of my brother, his friends, and many young men of that era. They were the Bigger Thomases of their day.

Rainey, Ma—Legendary blues singer who once challenged the Ku Klux Klan, had many imitators, made a short film that is still seen today, perhaps reminiscent of an early music video about a woman who's had too much to drink and is singing about the loss of love.

Randolph, A. Philip—Dignified, militant Negro leader and founder of the Brotherhood of Sleeping Car Porters.

Robinson, Jackie—First Negro to break the race barrier in American baseball. Played for the Dodgers. In retirement, became a Vice President of the Chock Full O' Nuts corporation.

Scottsboro—Famous case in which a group of Negro men were accused of raping two white women and brought to trial in the town of Scottsboro, Alabama. It was the cause célèbre of the 1930s. Langston Hughes wrote about it and the Communist Party used it in their platform. Thomas Mann himself was supposed to have written a letter to one of the Scottsboro boys in jail.

Smith, Bessie—Another legendary blues singer.

Smith, David—Friend of Sam Cornish, uneducated, built like Li'l Abner in the comic strip, had a flair for creating folk tunes, playing guitar and creating authentic southern ballads. Prolific lover of women and an unrecognized leader in the civil rights movement.

Stokes, Carl—Mayor of Cleveland, Ohio.

Thomas, Bigger—Fictional character created by Richard Wright. The darker side of "Uncle Tom," he was "Bigger" Thomas. A product of American racism and, as Wright saw him, representative of a change in male behavior in Europe and America in whites as well as blacks. Bigger Thomas was more than just a Negro man, he was representative of a society that was drifting toward the Fascism that would lead us into World War II.

Till, Emmett—Negro youth who was murdered by white men in Money, Mississippi, for supposedly whistling at a white woman.

Toomer, Jean—Author of the novel *Cane*, an experimental fiction in the tradition of Sherwood Anderson, the Nick Adams stories of Ernest Hemingway, and other works of fiction that chronicle the move from the rural and small-town America into the modern era.

Tubman, Harriet—Ex-slave who fled north and became part of the Underground Railroad. Personally led slaves from the South to the North. Mean and determined, she carried a pistol and drove them mercilessly. "Move or die," was Harriet's motto.

Turner, Nat —Leader of early slave rebellion and best known as the subject of William Styron's controversial and magnificent *Confessions of Nat Turner*.

Waller, Fats—Fabulous Negro entertainer. My recollection of Fats Waller is of a nattily dressed man at the piano singing and winking at the audience.

Wheatley, Phillis—American poetess and eighteenth century slave, poet, and translator, educated by her owners. George Washington was so impressed by her that he invited her to the White House and referred to her as "Miss Wheatley." Thomas Jefferson, however, was not impressed. Miss Wheatley married, which was unfortunate, as few men were her equal.

Wright, Richard—The most influential Negro writer of the twentieth century. Wright wrote in the European tradition, highly influenced by Flaubert, Dostoyevsky, and American writers such as Theodore Dreiser. He used his character, Bigger Thomas, as a metaphor for the male psyche.

OTHER BOOKS IN THE
NOTABLE VOICES SERIES

CAVANKERRY'S MISSION

Through publishing and programming, CavanKerry Press connects communities of writers with communities of readers. We publish poetry that reaches from the page to include the reader, by the finest new and established contemporary writers. Our programming brings our books and our poets to people where they live, cultivating new audiences and nourishing established ones